There is a River

*A Seven Week Guide for
Deepening Your Walk with God*

Dan Lemburg

CommuningWithGod.org

WESTBOW
PRESS®
A DIVISION OF THOMAS NELSON
& ZONDERVAN

WestBow Press books may be ordered through booksellers or by contacting:

WestBow Press
A Division of Thomas Nelson & Zondervan
1663 Liberty Drive
Bloomington, IN 47403
www.westbowpress.com
844-714-3454

Scripture quotations are taken from the New American Standard Bible® (NASB), Copyright © 1960, 1962, 1963, 1968, 1971, 1972, 1973, 1975, 1977, 1995 by The Lockman Foundation Used by permission. www.Lockman.org

ISBN: 978-1-6642-8879-9 (sc)
ISBN: 978-1-6642-8878-2 (e)

Library of Congress Control Number: 2023900322

Print information available on the last page.

WestBow Press rev. date: 2/15/2023

Foreword

There is a River is an extension of the ministry of **CommuningWithGod.org**, whose core objective is, "Leading believers into a lifestyle of communing with God for the purpose of building greater intimacy with Him."

Ephesians 3:16—19 depicts the apostle Paul's heartfelt prayer for every follower of Christ:

> "That He would grant you, according to the riches of His glory, to be strengthened with power through His Spirit in the inner man,
>
> so that Christ may dwell in your hearts through faith; and that you, being rooted and grounded in love,
>
> may be able comprehend with all the saints what is the breadth and length and height and depth,
>
> and to know the love of Christ surpasses knowledge, that you may be filled up to all the fulness of God."

We are convinced that this is Jesus's purpose and calling for every Christian. This book is dedicated to that end. May the Spirit of God enrich your life in Jesus through this study.

Week 1

Our story begins with an extraordinary individual, a dynamic prophet of God named Ezekiel. In Ezekiel's day God was dealing with flagrant disobedience in His chosen people by allowing Jerusalem to be conquered by the infamous king of Babylon, Nebuchadnezzar, who killed the majority of the populace and then uprooted and took captive the survivors into Babylon. Ezekiel lived among these exiles. It would be hard not to think of him as really exceptional since he received vision after vision—some dealing with future events and others revealing God's heart, His intent and purpose for all who call on His name.

Prior to Babylon's invasion of Jerusalem, God's temple— the first temple—had stood for some four hundred years. King Solomon constructed it over the course of several years, all aided by the foresight of his father, King David, who had gathered an enormous hoard of materials, the finest to be found anywhere. Foremost among these resources was a vast reserve of gold, silver and precious stones. It was magnificent, an edifice whose glory eclipsed that of any of its kind throughout the world! Its inner walls and floors were overlaid with pure gold and the whole place was furnished with priceless treasures. But all this splendor was negligible compared to its true purpose: it was inhabited by the Spirit of God Himself, a gem beyond description in the hearts and minds of the people of Israel—a house of honor and sacrifice to the one who chose Israel as His own possession.

Yet because in God's eyes "to obey is better than sacrifice" (1 Samuel 15:22), He allowed His holy temple to be ransacked and razed to its very foundation. The destruction of this gift of God was a tragedy for Israel beyond anything we can imagine.

The impact of this catastrophe on the Israelites has few comparisons in our generation. Who will ever forget the sadness we felt as we watched New Yorkers, dust covered, faces full of fear and anguish, even terror, fleeing the Twin Towers as they crumbled to the ground? Yet even the enormity of this heartbreak pales in comparison to what the people of Israel must have experienced as they saw their neighbors slaughtered, their city burned, God's temple destroyed and the escaping remnant trudging into captivity in a foreign land.

I'm sure the Holocaust that the Jewish people suffered under the terror of the Nazis was equal in scope, as well as other genocides and wars we have heard about. But even so, it is impossible to fully empathize since we have not had to experience such trauma personally.

In the fortieth chapter of the Old Testament book which is called by his name, Ezekiel tells of being brought out of captivity back to the land of Israel. He was miraculously taken to a mountain where he encountered a man with a measuring rod in his hand. In Ezekiel's vision the man set about documenting the measurements of a massive new temple. This temple complex was never to be built. It's obvious why: its size dwarfed both the former temple destroyed by the Babylonians and the second temple which was rebuilt by the returning exiles decades later.

Yet there it was in his vision, depicted in meticulous detail. Apparently, the image he saw was a symbol of a veiled spiritual truth concerning the kingdom of God, one that can only be understood through spiritual revelation.

Moving on to the forty-seventh chapter, Ezekiel describes a door of the temple, facing east. Water was flowing from under the threshold of this door, which is where the substance of our story takes shape.

Water, and what it symbolizes, is a recurring theme in the Bible. And why not? Is there anything remotely like it? We all must have water in order to survive. It is a key sustainer of life not only for us but for all living things. What better analogy might God have employed to explain the promise of the kind of life—His life, eternal life—which He has prepared for us?

Water! An unparalleled symbol of Christ's spiritual lifeblood poured out upon His chosen ones:

> There is a river whose streams make glad the city of God, the holy dwelling places of the Most High. God is in the midst of her, she will not be moved; God will help her when the morning dawns. (Psalm 46:4—5)

> Jesus said to the woman at the well, "If you knew the gift of God, and who it is who says to you, 'Give Me a drink,' you would have asked Him, and He would have given you living water.... Whoever drinks of the water that I will give him will become in him a well springing up to eternal life." (John 4:10, 14)

> Now on the last day, the great day of the feast, Jesus stood and cried out, saying, "If anyone is thirsty, let him come to me and drink. He who believes in Me, as the Scripture said, 'From his innermost being will flow rivers of living water.'" (John 7:37, 38)

Getting wet all over, without and within, an immersion in God's Spirit until rivers of living water actually flow out of your heart. This is what your Creator designed you for. This is His purpose for you. This is your heritage in Christ Jesus.

Now, coming back to Ezekiel's vision of water flowing from under the doorway of the temple, he begins to paint a picture:

> He brought me out by way of the north gate and led me around on the outside of the outer gate by way of the gate that faces east. And behold, water trickling out from the south side [of the temple]. (Ezekiel 47:2)

Notice here that both *bringing* and *leading* are mentioned. Who was this man? Was he an angel? Or was he the Spirit of Christ Himself? This question cannot be answered. But what is important is that Ezekiel was both brought out—in our case, "He delivered us out of the domain of darkness and transferred us to the kingdom of His beloved Son" (Colossians 1:13)—and then led. One cannot be led unless one is willing to follow: "For all who are being led by the Spirit of God, these are the sons of God" (Romans 8:14).

As children of the living God, we have been brought out of this world into all that God has prepared for those who love Him. But this mighty salvation is much more than one and done. The Scripture talks about a lifelong "obedience of faith" (Romans 1:5, 16:26), and this is where first being willing to be led and then courageously stepping forward becomes vitally important.

Reflection and Discussion
Week 1

Day 1

If it were not for the purpose of predicting the construction of a new temple, why would God give Ezekiel such a prophetic vision? What is the significance of a temple in the first place, and how does this differ from what God ultimately intended for His people in Christ Jesus (see Ephesians 2:19—22)? What other scriptures speak of this?

Day 2

Why would God use an idol-worshiping heathen king to bring His judgment upon Israel instead of doing it all by Himself? Knowing that honor and saving face were then, and are today, fundamental elements of Middle Eastern culture difficult to fully grasp by Westerners, was humiliation the goal? Was God merely breaking their pride? Or was His purpose also to preserve a remnant (see Romans 9:27—29)?

Day 3

Flowing from under the doorway of the temple was water. Why water? Why not blood, since the Bible tells us that life is in the blood (Leviticus 17:14) and thus represents the reality of life in Christ? A relationship between water and blood can be seen in 1 John 5:6—8. What other symbols does God use in His Word to shed greater light on the nature of His person and power?

Day 4

Are you being led by the Spirit of God, or are you leading? The difference between the two is staggering. 2 Corinthians 13:5 instructs us to examine ourselves to see if Christ is indeed in us. Should not this vital principle also apply to being led by the Holy Spirit? How can you know whether you are passing this further test?

Day 5

The Bible tells us that obedience to God is the litmus test of our faith. In addition to those found in Romans, what other verses speak of the requirement to obey God? Obedience to what is found in scripture is always the priority, but have you also been called by Him to some special purpose that requires a unique level of obedience? If so, describe it.

Week 2

Most people shove aside any thought of a deeper purpose for their lives. They simply accept the fact that they have been born into this world and now have a life to be lived. Why ask a whole lot of questions—questions with little hope of being answered anyway? "Who am I? No, who am I really? Why this world and why am I here?" The answers lie engulfed in mystery.

Given not only the incredible complexity of our humanity but also the magnificent reality of the natural world around us, wouldn't it make sense to at least attempt to explore the meaning of it all? Why settle for simply taking it at face value? Some try, but it's a lot of extra work. Skating through life one day at a time is much simpler. We aren't lazy, of course, most of us, that is. We're certainly willing to make the effort to lay the foundation for a career we hope will cultivate a pleasant lifestyle—a means of creating the best possible outcome for what we hope will be a "fulfilling" life during our time here on earth. Yet so often it all boils down to "let us eat, drink, and be merry, for tomorrow we die," which isn't much of a system for the pursuit of profound transcendent truth.

Philosophers are the ones who typically ask these deeper questions, and theologians attempt to answer them. But isn't "Who am I?" the question we should all be asking? There are answers to *Why?* but they lie far beyond the experience of life through our natural senses. After all, our spiritual nature is the one asking! Purpose is what we all crave in our innermost being: "Am I here for a *purpose*?" There is a way to find out if we are willing to honestly ask, and then beyond that to intently listen.

Yes, we are here for a purpose, and not just *for* a purpose, but *with* purpose. Am I splitting hairs here? Not in the least, because *a purpose* implies that we should be "doing something" while *with purpose* speaks of "being someone."

This, of course, implies the existence of a Creator—one who is far from impersonal; one who is intimately involved in every detail of our lives. And if He is in fact involved to that extent, there must also be a way of not only knowing about Him but also knowing Him on a personal level.

God reveals Himself as a person, a person we can get to know much like we can know anyone else. But how? Inquiring into what the Bible has to say is our primary source. In its pages we find a history of God's dealings with people just like us, all recorded for our benefit so that we might both understand God and be instructed as to how to live our lives in a manner pleasing to Him. The Bible is not only a narrative about God, it is the revelation of the nature of God Himself.

Those who have "found" God have come to this awareness not by gathering a set of facts. Rather God has "found" them. Their knowledge of God is the result of revelation, not solely from investigation. Yes, He will lead those who inquire into knowledge, but coming to actually know Him ultimately is His doing, not ours. We need to get over the idea that receiving Jesus as Lord and Savior is primarily a matter of inviting Jesus into our life, although there certainly is a meaningful element of that. Rather, He is inviting us into His (John 1:12, 13).

The first thing we need to understand is that God has a dynamic purpose for all He has created—all revolving around those He has chosen to share eternal life with Him. We call it Heaven which, sadly, has been thought of through the ages not only as an extravagantly blissful existence, but also a placid and idle one. Yet how could being eternally joined with such an explosively creative God be anything other than an adventure far beyond our wildest dreams?

God will explode into your life if you let Him. Let's get personal here for a moment. You have been created by a formidable God, one who is all-knowing and all-powerful, and capable of sustaining a universe so vast that even our most powerful telescopes cannot grasp its immensity. But why *you*? Why would God create *you* for such purpose? The Bible talks about your being in the mind of God before the foundation of the earth was laid (Ephesians 1:4), and then being intimately conceived:

> For You formed my inward parts;
> You wove me in my mother's womb.
> I will give thanks to You, for I am fearfully and
>   wonderfully made.
> Wonderful are Your works, and my soul knows
>   it very well.
> My frame was not hidden from You,
> When I was made in secret,
> And skillfully wrought in the depths of the earth;
> Your eyes have seen my unformed substance;
> And in your book were all written
> The days that were ordained for me,
> When as yet there was not one of them.
> (Psalm 139:13—16)

If this does not characterize the uniqueness of your individuality, I don't know what could! Extraordinary, cherished, beloved, significant—*priceless*, really. These descriptions merely scratch the surface of your meaning to God. It is often said that if you were the only one ever created Jesus would have died for you. I've always considered this idea to be a bit preposterous but have now come to realize that it actually is true.

Circling back to Ezekiel 47 once again, he goes on to say in verse 3:

> When the man went out toward the east with a line in his hand, he measured a thousand cubits, and he led me through the water, water reaching the ankles.

In my mind, this can easily be seen as the moment of our personal salvation; getting your feet wet, so to speak. Here the promise of God is discovered. *There is a river,* and rivers always have a source. The *promise* of God is the underlying source for of all that exists. A promise? God's promise is this: you have been invited to become his child, not just in the sense that "we are all God's children" as it is so often said, but as His chosen one, one who is to share eternity with Him.

God has called you to life in Him through Christ Jesus. He is offering the supernatural—instant transformation, to be born again—now capable of experiencing His eternal kingdom here on earth (John 3:3). Scripture puts it this way, "If anyone is in Christ, he is a new creature; the old things have passed away; behold, new things have come" (2 Corinthians 5:17).

Transformation is the key point here—immeasurably more than a superficial makeover. That's His promise! Jesus is offering *transformation*; a revolutionary recreation of our personhood. And yet, as dynamic as this radical conversion is, it is only the beginning; a launching into all God has planned for you.

Reflection and Discussion
Week 2

Day 1

Most Christians have settled the question as to why we are here on earth. The Bible is full of information regarding God's purpose for His creation. But it is also true that most remain confused about their own individual purpose. "I just don't know what God wants from me; what am I supposed to be doing for Him?" Have you put yourself in a position to hear from Him? How so?

Day 2

Regarding purpose, have you looked beyond the notion of "doing *something*" to "being *someone*" in God's eyes? Is your life in Christ wrapped up in *doing* in order to establish your identity, or have you discovered that God has created you first to *be* His own, regardless of your performance? Practically speaking, how can you cement this truth into your life so that you can genuinely live it out?

Day 3

Knowing God on a personal level is an incomparable gift. And the Bible is our manual for intimacy with Him. Do you truly interact with God in your reading of scripture? Is it primarily a source for information and inspiration? Or has it become a source of revelation—that is, the Holy Spirit revealing truths about Jesus, spoken beyond head-knowledge right into your heart? Describe what you have *heard*.

Day 4

Do you perceive yourself as somewhat meaningless in God's kingdom; or the way God sees you—as *priceless*? How can your attitude be changed regarding this? Does your reading of Psalm 139:13—16 help clarify your worth to God? Can you see how this could have been written personally for you? Why do we so easily accept this truth for others but have such a difficult time applying it to ourselves?

Day 5

When we think about the concept of being converted from our old ways to a life of following Christ, we often think of it as a decision we make. But down through Church history the term conversion has always meant transformation: "If anyone is in Christ, he is a new creature"—a revolutionary *new being* (1 Corinthians 5:17). Do you see yourself in this light? What other passages in scripture speak of this truth?

Week 3

Due to the brazen unfaithfulness of His people, God had vacated the first temple just prior to its destruction. Ezekiel describes this crushingly sad event in Chapter 10. Here God is seen seated on His throne above the cherubim of whirling wheels, the same vision he first described in Chapter 1. We can't go into the full details of this revelation right now, but I encourage you to read the account. It is one of the most magnificent pictures of God's splendor in the entire Bible.

Chapter 43 tells the story of the Spirit of God once more filling and occupying the temple Ezekiel saw in his vision. And once again this same image of God's glory is revealed—the *Shekinah Glory*, which is the Hebrew name for the presence of God dwelling on earth: "this is the place of My throne and the place of the soles of My feet, where I will dwell forever" (Ezekiel 43:7).

Solomon fittingly discerned the true nature of God, as described in his dedication of the first temple: "But will God indeed dwell on the earth? Behold, heaven and the highest heaven cannot contain You, how much less this house which I have built!" (1 Kings 8:27). No temple can contain the Spirit of God. Just as the water flowed from below the door in Ezekiel's vision, the water must flow. What is this flow? It is the Holy Spirit Himself; the river is the Spirit of God.

Back to our text, the man continued to lead, and Ezekiel was willing to follow. What an awesome experience!

> Again he measured a thousand and led me
> through the water, water reaching the knees.
> (Ezekiel 47:4a)

What do you suppose Ezekiel experienced as he followed deeper into the river? What any of us would: "Hey, this water is putting pressure on me. This is no pond; this water is moving, and if I'm not careful it might take me right along with it!" And still the man led further.

> Again he measured a thousand and led me through
> the water, water reaching the loins. (Ezekiel 47:4b)

"Now this is getting serious! I can barely keep my balance! My feet don't want to stay planted on the river bottom." And yet the man led on.

> Again he measured a thousand; and it was a river
> I could not ford, for the water had risen, enough
> water to swim in, a river that could not be forded.
> (Ezekiel 47:5)

In fact, if the man were to lead Ezekiel any further, he simply would have been swept away by the current. He knew there was a decision to be made at this point, and apparently so did the man.

> He said to me, "Son of man, have you seen this?"
> Then he brought me back to the bank of the river.
> (Ezekiel 47:6)

Now, a question arises here. Was the river ever intended to be crossed? Or was it meant to be swam in? Ezekiel may have been led back to the bank to consider this extremely important question. "It's obvious I can't ford the river, but what if I were to swim? Where would I end up? Way downstream? Would I drown?" Indecision brought on by our inborn self-interest is what we seem to be witnessing here. Self-interest sounds like such a selfish thing. But in this case, we are talking not about self-centeredness but merely the "fight or flight" syndrome natural to our humanity—a defense mechanism called self-preservation common to us all.

But there is even a bigger issue at play here—one absolutely fundamental to our being. It brings us right back to our previous question: "*Why? Who am I and why am I here?*" Let's start with the fact that every human being who has ever existed was created in the image of God. In the book of Genesis, God's intention for man, his purpose, is brought to light: "Let Us make man in Our image, according to Our likeness" (Genesis 1:26*a*). It's interesting that this verse gives us a first look not only into the nature of man, but also into the nature of God Himself: *"Us, Our image?"*

What about human nature? Our physical nature is not only being described here, but also the core of our being—our spiritual nature. If you have indeed been made in God's image, this can only mean that He also has a purpose for your life; purpose with immense significance. Would He not then need to communicate this with you? Yes, of course! And He's been doing so, even as early as the womb.

The Holy Spirit continues to speak this intimate truth to you today. It's declared throughout the Bible as *calling*. "I have called you by name; you are Mine" (Isaiah 43:1*b*). This obviously applies not only to the physical descendants of Abraham, but to all who have been born into relationship with God through Jesus our Lord: "It is not the children of the flesh who are children of God, but the children of the promise are regarded as descendants" (Romans 9:8).

Even though "calling" is one of the most talked about concepts in the Word of God, it is frequently misunderstood. The fact is, God's calling has been happening all your life. God has designed you as His own precious possession. This is why He created you; this is why you are here—to come to know Him and ultimately to be joined with Him for eternity. Open wide the ears of your heart, He is calling even now! And His call is not as subtle as you might think, "Wisdom shouts in the street," Proverbs 1:20 proclaims! What, or rather Who, is this *wisdom*? "But to those who are called, both Jews and Greeks, Christ the power of God and the wisdom of God" (1 Corinthians 1:24).

How does His *calling* play out in the lives of those who already have come to know Jesus as their Savior? "I know I'm saved. I know He has called me and that I'm now a child of God." Yet this fact does not mean His ongoing touch in your life somehow dissipates over time: Still He calls. And this brings us right back to the compelling reality Ezekiel faced at the bank of the river.

Now, at this point you might be wondering whether you have begun to follow Jesus into the river at all. Have you come to the place of experiencing the Spirit's flow against your legs to the knees or upward? Most likely you have if you are indeed feeling the tug of the Holy Spirit to go deeper with Him. Maybe you just haven't thought about it in the terms Ezekiel is describing here. Well, read on; there's a whole lot more to take into consideration.

Reflection and Discussion
Week 3

Day 1

Disobedience is evidence of the absence of belief (Hebrews 3:18,19). "If you will believe, you will see the glory of God," Jesus told Martha (John 11:40). *"If you will believe"* is a concept repeated in the Bible time and again. Where else do you find it in scripture? Can you identify passages where the instruction to *believe* is coupled with the command to *obey*?

Day 2

Some four hundred years elapsed from the time God's Shekinah Glory first inhabited Solomon's temple and the moment He departed. The books of Kings and Chronicles give a depressing account of what happened in between. Why does God allow disobedience (lawlessness) to go on so long before executing judgment? Is this a display of His lovingkindness and patience? Where else in the Bible do we find this occurring? And what does this say about His enduring love and acceptance for you?

Day 3

Are you allowing the Holy Spirit to lead you into His river? When was the last time you desired a deeper walk with God? What changes would have to occur in your life in order to experience a continuous overflow of Christ's Spirit? Are you willing to be led knee deep? How about further? What elements of your nature are resisting it?

Day 4

Was the river of the Spirit meant to be swam in? Have you thought about this? Are you considering the possibility? How would surrendering your life to God in this manner change the way you live your life? Do you sense anxiety in the same way you may have experienced fear over asking Jesus to take charge of your life in the first place? Are you alarmed at the prospect of further losing control?

Day 5

In what way does being created "in the image of God" drive you toward intimacy with Him—as suggested by Ezekiel's River? What about *calling*? Have you sensed the Holy Spirit's calling to greater nearness in your walk with Jesus? In what way have you felt it? Do you understand it; can you describe it?

Week 4

Why the river? Remember, we are not talking about any old river here. This is the river of the Spirit of God! And the Spirit calls. His call is much more than idyllic. Like a great river, He is flowing, flowing hard, an almost inescapable force. Can it be ignored? Is it possible simply to walk along its bank, appreciating its beauty yet never fully participating in its actual purpose? Millions do, every day. And millions more dip a toe or two to test the temperature.

The very presence of the river implies an invitation to dive on in, to experience all God has designed you for. Still, even though He knows what is best He will not force you into anything. He merely lays the opportunity before you, subtle in nature yet very tangible all the same. It just takes meaningful investigation into His Word, the Bible, along with a sincere openness of heart and pursuit of His will to begin to recognize His calling—just like Elijah heard the voice of God on Mount Sinai in 1 Kings 19:11—19: *"a sound of a gentle blowing (NASB), a still small voice (KJV), a gentle whisper (ESV, NIV)."*

Ezekiel obviously was a whole lot further along in his walk with God than most of us are. Still, he seemed to be facing a dilemma. Apparently, God had not commanded him to jump in and swim. Rather, it appears that God was presenting him with an opportunity. And not just an opportunity, but a *promise*.

Now when I had returned, behold, on the bank of the river there were very many trees on the one side and on the other.

Then he said to me, "These waters go out toward the eastern region and go down to the Arabah; then they go toward the sea, being made to flow into the sea, and the waters of the sea become fresh.

It will come about that every living creature which swarms in every place where the river goes, will live. And there will be very many fish, for these waters go there and the others become fresh; so everything will live where the water goes.

And it will come about that fishermen will stand beside it; from Engedi to Eneglaim there will be a place for the spreading of nets. Their fish will be according to their kinds, like the fish of the Great Sea, very many. (Ezekiel 47:7—10)

What is being portrayed here is *life*, and life more abundantly (John 10:10). But what does the experience of that life really mean? Here it seems that the river is both the giver and sustainer of abundant life. "Swarms of living creatures...very many fish" speaks of abundant provision supplying everything a person could ever need for a vital and healthy life. This is why the passage talks about fishermen joining in this profusion of wealth. For any fisherman there is nothing like a catch—not just a few, but a real catch, lots of fish!

The trees, rooted along the banks of the river are also a picture of abundant life (see also Psalm 1:3). Not only do they speak of lush beauty but also refreshing and comfort—what fisherman would not rather take refuge in the shade of a luxuriant tree than stand laboring under the hot sun?

This river is a driving force, ample in volume to make fresh the waters of the Dead Sea as far south as Engedi—no small distance from where the river first entered its waters. If you've had the privilege of visiting the Dead Sea and tried to swim—that is, to *float*—in its briny waters, you will immediately understand how miraculous a fresh water intrusion this far south would actually be.

All this is a marvelous picture of abundant life! But what was Jesus actually referring to in John 10:10 when He said, "I came that they may have life, and life more abundantly?" Was He speaking of temporal enrichment and comfort, or was He declaring a spiritual union with Himself meant to be fully experienced during our lifetime here on earth? Both Jesus's promise and Ezekiel's penetrating portrayal of the river of the Spirit unquestionably speak of the latter.

But the question is how we might walk out our life in Christ to its fully intended purpose. It's obvious that we were meant not only to appreciate and participate in the benefits of the river, but to swim, because "everything will live where the water goes." But how? Immersion is the key. "Come swim in the river of God," the Holy Spirit encourages. This opportunity—this *promise*—lies right before you. *There is a River*; the Spirit of God is calling! It's what you have been created for: Communing with God, intimate fellowship with your Creator which can be experienced in no other way.

Begin to immerse yourself in the Spirit of God. Scripture is full of examples of this happening in people's lives. Yes, these biblical lives were extraordinary, so remarkable that we can hardly imagine our own ever approaching such richness and purpose. Yet, "Whatever was written in earlier times was written for our instruction, so that through perseverance and encouragement of the Scriptures we might have hope" (Romans 15:4). Their lives are an example of God's promise that all who follow Him, "can know the love of Christ which surpasses knowledge, that you may be filled up to all the fulness of God" (Ephesians 3:19).

Now, rest assured that each and every one who has committed their life to Jesus enjoys the presence the Holy Spirit abiding within:

> In Him, you also, after listening to the message of truth, the gospel of your salvation—having also believed, you were sealed in Him with the Holy Spirit of promise, who is given as a pledge of our inheritance, with a view to the redemption of God's own possession, to the praise of His glory. (Ephesians 1:13, 14)

As wonderful as this promise is, does it end there? Is this the entire meaning of immersion in the river of the Spirit? Or is there something more to be anticipated from this incredible life in Christ which we have been privileged to enter? What does the Bible have to say about this extremely important question?

The Word of God tells us that there is indeed more to be hoped for in our relationship with Jesus—an actual baptism in the Holy Spirit. Some describe this as a further infilling of the Spirit, being *filled* with the Holy Spirit. The question is how it happens. Scripture portrays it as a further event experienced subsequent to being saved. Just as Jesus promised, the Holy Spirit fell on His disciples as they waited in the upper room following His ascension into heaven (Acts 2:4). For others it happened at the moment of their salvation experience, as in the case of Cornelius and his household (Acts 10:44—47). And still others were filled with the Spirit as Paul laid hands on them some time after becoming disciples of Jesus (Acts 19:1—7). In each case, being filled with the Spirit was accompanied by speaking with tongues.

Swimming in the river of God kind of sounds like being baptized. But there is a vast difference between water baptism and Spirit baptism. First of all, water baptism is commanded by God as a symbol of dying to our old man as we are immersed in water, and then rising anew into God's life as we come up from the water (Romans 6:3—5). It is an outward expression of an inward reality, commanded by the Lord as a tangible witness of His grace both to ourselves and to others.

On the other hand, immersion in the Holy Spirit as portrayed in Ezekiel doesn't feel like a command but more like an invitation, an opportunity, a promise—one which we may either pursue, put off, or simply ignore. It seems we have been given a choice in the matter.

Reflection and Discussion
Week 4

Day 1

What was your initial reaction to Jesus's words in John 10:10, "I came that they may have life, and life more abundantly?" Did it instill hope in you for prosperity and health for your life here on earth? This conclusion is almost unavoidable given the affluent consumer-driven society we tend to put our hope in. What did Jesus actually mean, and why is it important to your perception of the kingdom of God?

Day 2

Is prosperity to be expected for our life in Christ, or should we be minimalists? Is money evil? Is it an addiction, or merely a distraction? What do 2 Corinthians 4:16—18 and Colossians 3:1—4 say about where our focus should be? What other verses speak of the dynamic tension between earthly pursuits and kingdom mindedness?

Day 3

How might we walk out our life in Christ to its fully intended purpose? Is immersion in the river of the Holy Spirit really the key? If so, how can you not only dive in but also stay immersed in its powerful current? Why is this to be thought of not only as an opportunity but truly as God's *promise*? What's the difference between the two?

Day 4

Why does God keep Himself hidden from our earthly sight? And when He does speak into our heart, why does He communicate in such hushed tones? If His *calling* is so crucial, why not just come out and say it in such a way we can clearly understand? In what way does "for we walk by faith and not by sight" (2 Corinthians 5:7) play such an important role to our walk with Jesus?

Day 5

Does the word *expectation* have a place in your spiritual vocabulary? Or have you learned to be content with the status quo. Have you considered the offer of Jesus's promise of baptism in the Holy Spirit as a possibility? What about anticipation with the intention of pursuit? What might you stand to lose if you experienced such an immersion in the Spirit?

Do you find the suggestion of greater intimacy with Jesus somewhat disturbing?

Week 5

Once we are saved, we are called to a path of spiritual growth—not as an option but as a necessity. God has created us for an eternal purpose, which means He must have a specific plan for our life. To discover His purpose, intimate relationship with Him needs to be pursued. But since we are human, we naturally tend toward a shallow relationship as we go about our daily lives. Truth be told, it's far more comfortable than pursuing intimacy. Our flesh would much rather be involved with Christ merely as some sort of addition to our life. Yet look at it from God's perspective. Has He created us for an earthly life only, leaning on Him merely when we have needs, kind of like accessing an APP on a smart phone? We shouldn't be too surprised by such superficiality; we are effortlessly compelled by our nature.

Spiritual growth means living a fruitful life. The apostle Paul makes this very clear:

> "Therefore, my brethren, you also were made to die to the Law through the body of Christ, so that you might be joined to another, to Him who was raised from the dead, in order that we might bear fruit for God" (Romans 7:4).

The wonderful thing is that bearing fruit just happens naturally when we are bonded with Jesus: "I am the vine, you are the branches; he who abides in Me and I in him, he bears much fruit, for apart from Me you can do nothing" (John 15:5). "Our business is to concur with God; His alone is to originate," a wise old saint once wrote.

Jesus has given us every tool necessary to foster our spiritual growth. Immersion in His Spirit provides the power to do so. What did Jesus say to His disciples? "You will receive power when the Holy Spirit has come upon you" (Acts 1:8). This promise dealt specifically with the power to be His witnesses, but more broadly it is the power to, "walk in a manner worthy of the Lord, to please Him in all respects" (Colossians 1:10a). And this can only be achieved as we open ourselves up to Him. It's not so much a matter of changing as it is being changed.

Immersion in the power of the Holy Spirit opens wide the doorway for spiritual gifts to operate in and through you (1 Corinthian 12:1—11). Let's talk about this for a moment. What is the significance of spiritual gifts? They are tools: "But to each one is given the manifestation of the Spirit for the common good" (verse 7). Time does not allow us to explore each of the nine miraculous giftings mentioned in this passage. Nor does it serve the purpose of this study to do so. Each gifting has its place and time. Each is the power of God displaying itself through us.

One of these gifts, though, unquestionably has a critical bearing on the subject at hand. It is one many Christians would rather not think about, much less discuss: the gift of tongues. Yet it is important that we do so because it carries such purposeful meaning for Ezekiel's River of the Spirit. How so?

Verse 10 of Corinthians describes the gift of tongues as being "various kinds of tongues." The explanation of this verse is often thought of as meaning various languages. But that is not actually the case. Rather, "kinds of tongues" means types of tongues, not the languages themselves. There is a prophetic type of tongue, one that requires an interpretation for the purpose of benefiting the church. And there is a personal prayer language given solely for the benefit of the one using it: "For one who speaks in a tongue does not speak to men but to God; for no one understands, but in his spirit he speaks mysteries" (1 Corinthians 14:2). Further, "One who speaks in a tongue edifies himself" (1 Corinthians 14:4)—that is, builds himself up spiritually.

This can't help but bring up a very pertinent question, "If I don't understand what I am praying, what possible good is it?" "My *spirit* prays" is the answer, not my intellect (1 Corinthians 14:14,15). It is spirit to Spirit communication. And it's the kind that Jesus Himself said God desires: "But an hour is coming, and now is, when the true worshipers will worship the Father in spirit and truth; for such people the Father seeks to be His worshipers" (John 4:23). Can you see how important this kind of communication, this personal spirit to Spirit interaction with God, is? What a tool to maintain our saturation in the Holy Spirit. Think of it as empowering your swim in the river of God!

This spirit to Spirit interaction is actually a two-way street which also fosters a *Spirit to spirit* exchange. That is, it opens wide the door for God speaking back. There is nothing like feeling the presence of the Lord, and "praying in the Spirit"—as it is often described in Scripture—is a means of experiencing this delightful outcome.

The issue of praying in tongues having been addressed, there is one question that remains: "What if I fail to experience the gift of a prayer language in my walk with Jesus? Am I in some way deficient?" I think we can all agree that throughout the history of the church there are numerous examples of believers who have not exercised the gift of tongues and yet have borne incredible fruit in their lives. Communing with God is the key; any attempt we make toward that end is what matters. No one has accomplished anything meaningful in the kingdom of God without daily spending time in the pursuit of intimacy with Him, just as king David so insightfully expressed:

Give ear to my words. O Lord, consider my
   groaning.
Heed the sound of my cry for help, my King and
   my God; for to You I pray.
In the morning, O Lord, You will hear my voice;
In the morning I will order my prayer to You and
   eagerly watch. (Psalm 5:1—3)

Even so, there is no denying that God has given the gift of praying in the Spirit for a strategic and useful purpose. Otherwise, why bother? So, we must not let confusion over it keep us from reaching for all God has promised in His Word. Our pursuit of God demands it. "What is the outcome then? I will pray with the spirit, and I will pray with the mind also; I will sing with the spirit and I will sing with the mind also" (1 Corinthians 14:15).

How can I receive this gift? "Ask! How much more will your heavenly Father give the Holy Spirit to those who ask Him" (Luke 11:9—13). And *keep asking*, as the tense of the Greek verb actually suggests—*keep seeking, keep knocking*.

Equally important is the fact that God wants us to persevere in our pursuit of Him and His spiritual gifts. Did Jesus not say, "all things for which you pray and ask, believe that you have received them, and they will be granted you" (Mark 11:24)? Step boldly forth and believe God for what He has promised. Faith is what He is looking for!

Reflection and Discussion
Week 5

Day 1

Think about how much you have changed since deciding to put your trust in the Lord Jesus. Having found that you are bearing some fruit for God, are you content in your walk with Him? Do you feel a tug for more? Have you asked the Holy Spirit to plant a greater thirst for Jesus within you?

Day 2

What is your connection with Jesus like? Being firmly joined to the vine allows God's vital nutrients to flow. Has your union with Jesus resulted in bearing fruit effortlessly, or do you find yourself striving to grow that fruit? Have you discovered that a vibrant bond with Him the key to genuine fruitfulness? What obstacles in your life are preventing you from experiencing an *immersion* in God's Spirit?

Day 3

What's your reaction when reading about the spiritual gifts listed in 1 Corinthians 12:1—11? Do you think they are for you, or for someone else? It is often said that these giftings are no longer applicable for the church today—that they have ceased to be necessary now that the Church is established. Is this true, or is it merely an excuse? Examine yourself; do you feel powerless without them?

Day 4

Have you experienced the gift of praying in tongues through the baptism in the Holy Spirit?

If so, how has it empowered your intimacy with God? If not, do you think it could help?

What has been your reaction when encountering the demonstration of this gift during a church meeting? Has it revulsed you, or attracted you? Have you witnessed this gift being used in an imbalanced manner? If so, how has it colored your perception?

Day 5

What is your prayer life like? I hesitate to ask this embarrassing question because the answer so often is, "Well, it could be better," usually meaning it is pretty much nonexistent.

It's a common problem, even though the Bible expresses the need for prayer so emphatically. Jesus has created you to *commune* with Him. How might opening yourself up to the idea of receiving a personal prayer language help enable it?

Week 6

The truths we've just discussed become all the more important since there are serious impediments to spiritual growth standing in our way. Any mature believer will tell you this very thing. The lesson of Ezekiel's River of the Spirit also addresses it head-on:

> But its swamps and marshes will not become fresh; they will be left for salt. (Ezekiel 47:11)

Have you ever noticed that in every river there are eddies? What is an eddy? It is a swirling backflow next to the bank caused by the stream hitting some kind of obstacle. When the current encounters such a blockage, most of the river runs past while some of the water backs up into sort of a pond. Throw a leaf in and you will see it rotate around and around. Now some of this swirling water will eventually reenter the mainstream of the river, but some of it will not. If there is a low spot on the bank, water will escape into a marsh and stagnate. There is no outlet for water trapped in a marsh.

Likewise, there will always be obstacles to the flow of the Spirit in your life. One might consider such an impediment as a blockage or as a challenge. Either way, it results in being trapped at least temporarily, or much worse permanently. This problem is often described as being in a valley, where it becomes difficult to sense the uplifting presence of God. We all want to live on the spiritual mountaintop, but that's simply not the nature of relationship with God.

These valleys—trials and tribulation as the Bible often puts it—are places of suffering which can boil down to an irritating stall in our spiritual progress. Suffering may come in many forms: physical, emotional, relational, spiritual, financial, persecution by others—you name it. If we see such obstacles as challenges and persevere, God always provides a path through them, just as water trapped in an eddy can be freed back into the river's flow. But if we give up, our spiritual life will ultimately end up in the marsh, stagnating and causing us to backslide.

To make matters worse, we must never discount the fact that our progress can fretfully be hindered by the presence of a powerful enemy, Satan and his minions: "For our struggle is not against flesh and blood, but against the rulers, against the powers, against the world forces of this darkness, against the spiritual forces of wickedness in the heavenly places" (read Ephesians 6:10—17 for the full story). God's direction here is simply to "stand firm" in the face of it.

And there is another trial brought on by the inherent weakness of human nature: "But each one is tempted when he is carried away and enticed by his own lust" (James 1:14). This is a challenge common to us all.

Do these headwinds in some way alleviate our responsibility to pursue intimacy with God? It might be easy to think so. The elements of suffering, demonic influence, and the power of our own flesh result in a potent brew hindering our pursuit of Jesus and all He has planned for us. What was God thinking when He subjected us to this world with all its powerful influences?

Choice is the answer to this logical question. Will you pursue spiritual growth in spite of it all? Or will you stagnate. You really do have a choice in the matter: "For we have become partakers of Christ, if we hold fast the beginning of our assurance firm until the end" (Hebrews 3:14). What we must understand is that, at the bottom of it all, God allows these barriers to exist in order to strengthen our resolve to pursue Him. In God's eyes our life here on earth is an incubator of sorts. He uses all types of circumstances to finish what He started, ultimately growing us into the kind of people He planned (Philippians 1:6).

We must choose a path—either obedience, or disobedience. Hebrews 3:12—14 talks about this very thing, describing the potential for hardening of the heart. The Israelites were meticulously instructed by God in His ways. He commanded their obedience if they were to inherit all He had planned for them. Nevertheless, they chose to disobey. It was a clear display of the rebellion which resides in the heart of all people. They watched God miraculously lead their exodus out of Egypt, and then audibly heard Him speak His law to them from Mount Sinai in a thunderous voice so violent that they begged that no further word be spoken to them. Yet having witnessed this phenomenal display of God's power, they were still willing, almost immediately, to rebel in disobedience!

We are quick to judge this shameless failure. At the same time, we who have experienced the Lord Jesus Christ, God incarnate, verifiably coming into our hearts and lives are still willing to shove Him aside—however subtle our personal rebellion might be. It wouldn't be so bad if He hadn't left us with a thorough New Testament account of who He is, all He has accomplished, and what He wants. Having so clearly revealed His will for our lives, illuminated by the presence of the Holy Spirit residing within, we are indeed left with little excuse but to obey Him. And yet we so often fail. Quite an indictment! It's a clearcut display of self-interest. But take heart; we're all in the same boat—self-absorption is bound up in our nature.

Consider what the writer says next: "To whom did He swear that they would not enter His rest, but to those who were disobedient? So we see that they were not able to enter because of unbelief" (Hebrews 3:18,19). He makes clear that disobedience is ultimately tied to the existence of *unbelief*. On the other hand, obedience demonstrates faith—faith that pleases God (Hebrews 11:6).

Disobedience is indeed a spiritual killer, but complacency is just as big a threat. This is an issue far more common to believers than outright defiance. And it's so easy to be lulled into since we naturally tend to get caught up in the pleasures and challenges of everyday life. Yet Jesus desires—no, demands, really—that we wholeheartedly pursue Him. Did He not say, "I know your deeds, that you are neither cold nor hot; I wish that you were cold or hot. So because you are lukewarm, and neither hot nor cold, I will spit you out of My mouth" (Revelation 3:15,16)? This in-your-face exhortation applies not only to the church in Laodicea, but to us all.

A.W. Tozer, one of the most prolific and insightful Bible teachers of the twentieth century, wrote this commentary concerning the human heart:

> I think the more we learn about God and His ways and of man and his nature we are bound to reach the conclusion that we are just about as holy as we want to be. We are just about as full of the Spirit as we want to be. The reason why many are still troubled, still seeking, still making little forward progress is because they have not yet come to the end of themselves.

"Do not grieve the Holy Spirit of God, by whom you were sealed for the day of redemption," Paul plainly tells us in Ephesians 4:30. The bottom line is where you stand in your pursuit of intimacy with Jesus. Are you living to please Him, or chasing a pointless cycle of self-gratification. The question is not, "where is God at in my life?" but, "where am I at in His?"

Despite these ever-present challenges, *there is a river*. And where the river of the Spirit flows there is hope: "and hope does not disappoint, because the love of God has been poured out within our hearts through the Holy Spirit who was given to us" (Romans 5:5) This is His promise of life, and life more abundantly.

Reflection and Discussion
Week 6

Day 1

Have you experienced being trapped in a spiritual swamp? If so, what was it like? What steps did you take to escape it? What should your encouragement be to those whom you see bogged down in their walk with God? Would you say, "Well, you'll get through it!" Or rather should you urge them to take purposeful steps to conquer it?

Day 2

What is your spiritual life like today? What obstacles have you encountered, or are presently encountering, in your progress toward spiritual growth? Describe how suffering, demonic opposition, or problems with the weakness of your nature may be contributing to frustration in your pursuit of God.

Day 3

Is outright disobedience to what you know God wants an issue? Or are you experiencing an attitude of complacency? Is it both? Embarrassment over bringing such issues to light before others can be very disturbing. The instruction found in James 5:16 is always a challenge, but how might it serve to break down pridefulness. How might prayer for one another be a healing solution?

Day 4

In what way has God communicated His will for your life? Why would God give us the ability to choose between our own way and His? Are you consistently studying His Word to uncover His truths? Has the Holy Spirit spoken to you by other means? How so? Describe how obedience has nurtured your life in the Spirit. How has disobedience served to derail it?

Day 5

Have you thoughtlessly "grieved the Holy Spirit of God" by settling for less than what He desires for your life? What is your reaction to Tozer's commentary on the human heart?

How likely is it to change this stubborn pattern in human nature? What steps do you need to take today toward the solution?

Week 7

Repetition in Scripture always amplifies the importance of what is being taught. Thus, the Lord wraps up Ezekiel's intense vision of the River of the Holy Spirit with one last verse—summarizing, and then expanding on His teaching to bring greater insight into His purpose and provision for His chosen ones:

> By the river on its bank, one side and on the other, will grow all kinds of trees for food. Their leaves will not wither and their fruit will not fail. They will bear every month because their water flows from the sanctuary, and their fruit will be for food and their leaves for healing. (Ezekiel 47:12)

The trees along the banks never lose their leaves and they never cease bearing fruit, because their roots are nourished by the ceaseless flow of life-giving moisture from the sanctuary—the eternal presence of God Himself. Nor will the Spirit of God ever cease to flow in and through our lives if we will simply cooperate with Him:

> Blessed is the man who trusts in the Lord
> And whose trust is in the Lord.
> For he will be like a tree planted by the water,
> That extends its roots by a stream

And will not fear when the heat comes;
But its leaves will be green,
And it will not be anxious in a year of drought
Nor cease to yield fruit. (Jeremiah 17:7—8)

With such a glorious opportunity at our fingertips, it's shocking that we could simply brush it aside. Or worse yet, ignore it altogether. Sadly, this sort of response to God's call is far too common. It's why we need to be reminded about what is truly important—that is, who we have been designed to be in the first place.

When asked by an expert in the Law what is the foremost commandment, Jesus responded, "You shall love the Lord your God with all your heart, and with all your soul, and with all your mind" (Matthew 22:37). What an answer! What could be more straightforward, more fundamental? And yet, with what we know about human nature, what could be harder! What might have been your reaction if you were the one standing before Jesus when He gave that stunning reply—you, who are often just as steeped in your own ways as that lawyer was in his? This is a key question we all need to consider.

Have you wondered why it is so difficult to carve out a portion of your day to quietly spend time with God? It seems almost impossible, doesn't it. As we get our day started, we would rather do almost anything else than be slowed down by seeking God. But Jesus Himself, the creator and sustainer of all things, has invited you into this kind of intimate fellowship with Himself. What's wrong with this picture—how could we possibly remain reticent? Well, we've already covered most of this ground. So, let's focus on solutions rather than trying to beat a dead nag.

What relationship has ever been built without first spending time together? Taking time to engage Jesus requires a desire to do so. And therein lies the problem—lack of desire. The question is, though, how I can change what has become so entrenched in my life. Appetite is the key. We have little appetite for spiritual things because we are human, and therefore just naturally have more desire for earthly things.

Have you thought about intimacy with God as an acquired taste? We see this play out in our children: "Daddy, let me taste your coffee," only to find them turning up their nose in disgust. Later on, of course, these same kids become avid drinkers like the rest of us. Somewhere along the line there was an adjustment in attitude, a change in appetite.

How can we go from rushing off to our own pursuits to carving out time for intimacy with Jesus? There's really only one way. Make it a priority, no matter how uncomfortable it might be. Then, seek the Holy Spirit's help. He's willing if you are! Start with a commitment to read your Bible with the intent of trusting the Holy Spirit to "guide you into all truth." After all, it's His purpose: "He will glorify Me, for He will take of Mine and disclose it to you," Jesus taught His disciples in John 16:13—15.

You need to give the Holy Spirit something to work with! And He will, ushering you into God's truth, if you present him with the opportunity to do so. He will indeed speak to you in His own subtle way, deeply instilling in you His will and His ways.

As you put this discipline into practice you will find your appetite for Jesus growing on its own. Why? Because there is simply nothing more satisfying than having the Holy Spirit speaking the eternal truths of God into your heart. He wants to reveal Himself to you; He wants you to grow. Stick with it and you will find spiritual gifts erupting in your life. You will become a different person in spite of yourself.

As you grow you will also find yourself less and less reluctant to submit yourself to further spiritual disciplines and giftings: prayer in its various forms, serving, teaching, giving liberally, leadership, showing mercy cheerfully, even prophetically speaking and exhorting others—all enabled by growth in your faith (Romans 12:6—8).

And we must never discount the importance of fellowship with other believers. This also is a cornerstone for spiritual growth. "So we, who are many, are one body in Christ, and individually members one of another" (Romans 12:5). Jesus is the head over His worldwide body of believers. But our participation starts at the local level. Stay involved!

Now even as growth in the Spirit becomes a normal part of our Christian life, we must guard our pursuit of God from becoming sterile—stale, shall we say. While initially this may not be a serious problem, it remains an issue. How many times while reading the Bible have my thoughts been diverted to anything other than what I should be concentrating on, even reading whole sections of scripture somewhat unconsciously. Or praying with an apparent lack of interest. Again, our nature is the culprit, and so we must intentionally combat indifference by staying immersed in the river of the Spirit.

A key element for success in your quiet time with God is a discipline few Christians want to hear about, much less explore in their lives: memorization of scripture. Why? Because it is hard, of course. Still, even though purposeful memorization is quite demanding, it's more than worth it. Beginning with recitation of what you've memorized can be extremely meaningful since it enhances meditation with Jesus during your time with Him. It certainly helps one's focus. Recalling what has been hidden in your heart provides a platform for the Holy Spirit to speak, especially when interspersed with praying in the Spirit. Try it. Start small and watch your desire for more to grow as your experience of God flourishes.

Throughout the Scripture we find pursuit of intimate relationship with God an ever-present theme. There simply is no way of getting around this core truth, even though our prosperous and consumer-driven culture confronts spiritual priorities at every turn. Jesus was adamant on this point: "Store up for yourselves treasures, not on earth but in heaven. For where your treasure is, there your heart will be also. But seek first His kingdom and His righteousness, and all these things will be added to you" (Matthew 6:19—21, 33).

Yes, we must be diligent. And we must also beware. Once we have begun to experience success in these spiritual disciplines we must remain on guard against an ever-present obstacle to our growth in the Spirit: spiritual pride. This is easy to fall into because the temptation to display our accomplishments before others is so natural to us. We must understand that such an attitude is repulsive to the Holy Spirit, as well as to others. Foremost in God's mind is our growth in humility. There are dozens and dozens of verses throughout the Bible dealing with this issue: "clothe yourselves with humility toward one another, for God is opposed to the proud, but gives grace to the humble" (1 Peter 5:5b).

Allow me to leave you with a final thought. God is extremely generous in His dealings with us. He has made provision for our lives at every turn: "Grace and peace be multiplied to you in the knowledge of God and of Jesus Christ our Lord; seeing that His divine power has granted to us everything pertaining to life and godliness, through the true knowledge of Him who called us by His own glory and excellence (2 Peter 1:2, 3).

As Oswald Chambers so insightfully wrote:

> Beware of anything that competes with loyalty to Jesus Christ. The greatest competitor of devotion to Jesus is service for Him. The one aim of the call of God is the satisfaction of God, not a call to do something for Him.
>
> The men and women Our Lord sends out on His enterprises are the ordinary human stuff, plus dominating devotion to Himself wrought by the Holy Spirit.

Reflection and Discussion
Week 7

Day 1

How does being planted beside the river of the Holy Spirit differ from swimming in it?

Either way we enjoy and gain from the life-giving nourishment He provides. Yet there is a profound difference. Have you considered the importance of diving into a deeper relationship with Jesus? Are you tired of dryness? If so, how willing are you to make the effort to get wet all over?

Day 2

Has carving out time from your busy day for meaningful interaction with God been an issue? What are you doing about it? Have you committed to consistently read the Word, or sought out a yearly Bible reading plan available on-line? How does prayer factor into your reading to keep things from becoming stale? What does intimacy with God really mean, and how might you see it grow?

Day 3

Have you experienced your appetite increasing for things in your life: certain foods, kinds of entertainment, travel, friendships and the like? Has your desire grown without first associating yourself with them? In what way might your relationship with God grow in like manner? Have you felt an urgency to spend time in order to "acquire a taste" for God's Spirit? Do you think Scripture memorization holds a key?

Day 4

What was your reaction upon hearing about the various spiritual giftings described in scripture? Have you considered that they might be for you, or are you concerned about these things becoming too deeply rooted in your life? Do you think they might be too costly, possibly interfering with your own plans and desires? What can be done to develop a more God-pleasing attitude?

Day 5

Many of us are naturally outgoing, thriving on interaction with others. Others are more introverted, reluctant to get involved. How can you overcome the obstacle to being in fellowship with other believers? What is God's purpose for it? Since it is impossible to build relationships merely by attending church, have you considered the value of becoming a member of a small group, or serving within the church?

Printed in the United States
by Baker & Taylor Publisher Services